The 13 Myths of Potty Training:

Realities and Simple Solutions

by

Sylvia Ford

Order this book online at www.trafford.com
or email orders@trafford.com

Most Trafford titles are also available at major online book retailers.

Author Credits: Illustrations by Douglas Beckner

Printed in the United States of America.

ISBN: 978-1-4120-6701-0 (sc)

Library of Congress Control Number: 2011901650

Trafford rev. 02/10/2011

 www.trafford.com

North America & international
toll-free: 1 888 232 4444 (USA & Canada)
phone: 250 383 6864 ♦ fax: 812 355 4082

Table of Contents

INTRODUCTION

The 13 Myths of Potty Training: Realities and Simple Solutions

There are so many misleading ideas about when and how a child should learn to use the toilet. Some believe children should initiate the process completely while others believe you can teach a child of nine months to eliminate in the right place at the right time.

Although we have no control over the child's physical ability to eliminate, we do have control over the environment and how the task is presented. I want to give you a mindset and a method that can help you maneuver through this task proactively and with respect for you and your child.

It's important you understand at the outset that I am not one of those people who believes that most children will initiate learning how to use the toilet when they are ready. I believe that children are too busy concentrating on everything else they are doing, like playing, to know when they should move forward in their development with using the toilet. Yes, their bodies do develop without their will, but their cognitive understanding about the task of using the toilet does not come naturally. This is where adults can take the lead and help children in developmentally appropriate ways that are beneficial to the child as a whole.

After running numerous of workshops on this topic, I have found that some parents are worried about pushing the child. So they wait until their child turns 4 only to finally give up on expecting the child to initiate the process. I am NOT in favor of pushing, which usually includes unrealistic expectations of the child, laced with shame-inducing tactics.

I DO promote providing the right equipment, attitude, and routine to help the child gain skills as their mind-body connection matures and develops. Learning to use the potty is not just a physical task: it requires thinking and emotional maturity too.

There comes a time when almost every child starts to resist because learning to stay dry is just not on their agenda. It's on THE ADULT'S agenda. So beginning potty training with your child before the age of approximately 2 years probably won't get your child trained "early". It may just set up unrealistic expectations. There's a time for everything and the realistic time to begin potty training for a typically developing child is 2 to 3 years, and they may not be out of diapers for sleep times until about 4 years of age. I favor starting a child at about 2.5 years old, knowing there will be some pretty predictable hurdles, including regression, along the way.

There is a good window of opportunity between the age of 2 and 3 when most children are usually physically ready to begin learning to use the toilet. As they approach 4, children are more difficult to distract and lead. By the time they are well into their 4th year, they have much more self-awareness and can become more embarrassed if they have accidents around their friends. That's one reason I think it's important to help children experience the task earlier than the age of 4, so they have time to practice and master most of it by the time they are into their 4th year (but 4 year-olds usually still need assistance with initiating and cleanup).

Children's development ebbs and flows, one step forward, a few steps back. It's a process that takes more than just a few weeks or months. The good news is that there are also many children who amaze us with how quickly they master the skills, even after being very reluctant in the beginning.

Resistance by children is typical but it's not the only thing that can make the process difficult. There are also many misconceptions about what is best when helping children learn to use the toilet -- I call these the 13 Myths of Potty Training. These myths make parents apprehensive about initiating the toilet-learning task with their child. Some parents feel that their hands are tied until the child stops rejecting the idea.

This book aims to replace the 13 myths with reality. Specific strategies are offered that take advantage of your child's human nature, and are intended to free you up so you can go forward in helping your child take this step of independence.

ONE: THE MYTHS AND REALITIES OF POTTY TRAINING

The 13 Myths of Potty Training

1. A child will let you know when they are ready to start the process.

2. If a child protests it means they are not ready.

3. Some children in other countries/from other cultures than the American culture learn to use the toilet by age one.

4. Being potty trained means a child can initiate her trip to the toilet, operate her own clothing, clean herself up when she's done and continue her play without any help from an adult.

5. Children learn to have bowel movements in the toilet before they learn to urinate in the toilet because bowel movements are more on a bodily "time clock".

6. If a child can dress and undress himself it means he is ready to use the toilet.

7. "Pull-ups" (disposable diapers with perforated sides) help a child learn to use the toilet.

8. Letting children run around naked helps them learn to use the toilet.

9. Once a child is out of diapers you should never go back to using them.

10. Reward systems always work and never hurt.

11. Pretending with a doll helps the child learn to use the toilet.

12. The longer a child sits on the toilet the more successful he/she will be.

13. If you do this RIGHT there won't be any accidents to clean up.

The Realities about Potty Training

Myth 1: *A child will tell you when they are ready to start the process.*
Reality: Knowing how to use the toilet is a self-help skill like brushing the teeth, nail-clipping, or hair washing. It's the adult's responsibility to initiate taking the child through the process until the activity is familiar and, gradually, more

initiated by the child. The child's inability to understand what is best for his own development makes it necessary for the adult to make the changes in the child's life that will lead the child to the next stage of maturity (children with developmental delays may take longer).

Myth 2: *Some children in other countries/from other cultures than the American culture learn to use the toilet by age one.*

Reality: In many cultures it is part of the cultural norm to begin sitting the child on a receptacle to eliminate before the age of one. But from experience, having been raised in one such culture, I know that the child does not become trained to know what to do and when to do it. It is the adult that trains *himself* to know the child's cues and timing. The biggest reality is that a child's physical development does not consistently allow her to know how to hold and eliminate at will consistently before the age of about 2 years old.

It often happens that in the toddler years (generally between 16 and 18 months) a child will actually urinate in the potty. The child might proceed successfully for about a week but almost definitely, this behavior will fade. This is a very common story, so when this happens with your child DON"T get your hopes up that your child will learn to use the toilet early. But DO be glad it is the very beginning of a process.

Myth 3: *If a child protests it means he/she is not ready.*

Reality: Children protest about all kinds of things. Would you allow your children to never bathe just because they protested about it? It is important to stay consistent by following through when it is called for. But staying consistent does not mean expecting the child to eliminate when YOU want them to. All you can do is stay consistent with the routine. The rest is up to the child. Do not assume your child is not ready because they are protesting. Two-and three-year-olds are known for their protests. It's ironic and fitting that learning how to use the potty naturally occurs when a child becomes much more conscious of wanting autonomy more than ever.

Myth 4: *Being potty trained means a child can initiate the trip to the toilet, operate their own clothing, clean up when they are done, and continue their play without any help from an adult.*

Reality: Young children's brains don't have the ability to juggle several tasks simultaneously. So when they are focused on their play, it's hard for them to switch gears right in the middle without your help. More likely you will be helping your child with many parts of the task--except the eliminating of course!

To me, being potty trained means the child is in underwear for most of the waking hours, urinating in the potty routinely, and finally pooping in the potty but still needing to be cleaned up. And it gets easier from there, but if you don't initiate and assist with the follow-through to the bathroom, your child may not be very successful. You need to be the guide. You need to prompt them, be consistent, and help the child to follow through with the routine, even if they don't eliminate.

Myth 5: *Children learn to have bowel movements in the toilet before they learn to urinate in the toilet because bowel movements are more on a bodily time clock.*

Reality: People are more on a "body clock" for bowel movements than they are for urinating, but most children learn to stay dry from urine before they learn to poop in the potty at will. Poops often happen in the potty when the child is trying to urinate, but mastering one's bowel movements comes between the age of 3 and 4. If a child is not yet three years old, I focus on helping them stay dry in their underwear. More information on bowel movements and using the diaper for this task is in Chapter Seven.

Myth 6: *If a child can dress and undress him/her self it means he/she is ready to use the toilet.*

Reality: Many children cannot dress and undress themselves, but they are ready to begin using the toilet. Some children who do know how to dress and undress themselves will go on strike when you need them to remove their pants to sit on the potty. For better follow-through, just help children with their clothes when needed and dress them in clothing that is easy to deal with, elastic waistbands -- no buttons, zippers, or suspenders. Don't gauge your child's readiness by their ability to dress or undress on their own.

Myth 7: *"Pull-ups" help a child learn to use the toilet.*

Reality: The diaper companies are making a lot of money with disposable diapers that children can more easily pull up on their own, disposable diapers that "let your child feel the wetness," disposable diapers that have superheroes that disappear when they get wet, and so on.

I think disposable diapers in general are very helpful! But please do not believe that these diaper gimmicks will help your child learn how to use the potty. If you don't have a child who thinks pulling her own diaper up and down is the best thing ever, then you should just use a regular (and cheaper) disposable. The same advice applies to the child who really WANTS to see the superhero disappear when it gets wet.

Disposable diapers with any gimmick are basically all exactly the same functionally -- they do their job well. They pull the moisture away from the skin so that after a while, the child feels comfortable in the soggy diaper. But a child may learn to make it to the toilet more consistently if she comes to realize that she does not like the feeling of being wet. This can only be learned by practicing in underwear. More about getting out of diapers in Chapters Two and Seven.

Myth 8: *Letting children run around naked helps them learn to use the toilet.*

Reality: This might help boys a little because they can see where the pee comes out from and that is interesting. But for girls, it may be difficult to know where things are coming from. I don't think running around naked helps children potty train. But it's fine to let them run around when it's convenient outdoors in warm weather. But, don't count on it to help your child learn how to use the toilet.

Myth 9: *Once a child is out of diapers, you should never go back to using them.*

Reality: It's not a good idea to keep switching back and forth from diaper to underwear and back to diaper again. But there IS a stage when children wear diapers and underwear at different times of the day. Generally the goal is always to move forward and slowly eliminate the need for diapers at all.

One appropriate time when a child may go back to using a diaper is usually during the third year. Children are often doing very well with staying dry in their underwear but they start to resist pooping in the potty. They insist on pooping in a diaper and some will wait until the nighttime diaper is put on to have their BM for the day. You may actually help the child progress if you allow the use of a diaper for BMs for a period of time -- see Chapter Seven.

Myth 10: *Reward systems always work and never hurt.*

Reality: Before the age of 4.5 it's very hard for most children to understand the building up of accomplishments over time, such using as a sticker chart. When they are young, children need the reward to be immediate and tangible. So a stamp or sticker on the hand is a good choice. The reward should be given just for trying on the potty, not necessarily only when they have eliminated.

One mother called me to ask why her 2.5 year-old son had started to reject the sticker chart, crying and saying he didn't want it. So she folded it up and put it in the garbage, which to her surprise made him cry harder. It's possible that he wanted to please her and knew that he could not always use the potty successfully, maybe he felt anxious about the failure and pressure the sticker chart represented to him and felt torn about it, whether it was on the wall or in the garbage.

Myth 11: *Pretending with a doll helps the child learn to use the toilet.*

Reality: For a minute let's consider neural networks and how they form. They require repetitive, patterned actions. Holding a doll over a potty teaches the child to get really good at holding the doll over the potty. He does not physically go through the motions that it takes to actually use the potty, so naturally those neural pathways for that pattern of actions are NOT being established in the brain. In my opinion, the doll thing is fun but not especially helpful in teaching children how to use the toilet themselves.

Myth 12: *The longer a child sits on the toilet the more successful he/she will be.*

Reality: If the child gets used to sitting for a very long time each time he sits on the potty, he learns that this task is both long and boring. Help him get used to sitting for at least 20 to 30 seconds and if he can't eliminate, he can be finished. Some children want to stay longer and that is their own choice because they can feel something happening in their body that makes them think they should wait a bit longer. If we make them sit for long periods of time they will learn to anticipate a long delay in their play and hate it when you say its time to "try".

Myth 13: *If you do this "RIGHT" there won't be any accidents to clean up.*

Reality: Let's just say... it isn't true. There WILL be accidents to clean up. Not going about things in a haphazard way is always helpful. Well thought-out plans do help keep the accidents to a minimum. But the accidents are part of the process of your child's learning.

 # Two: A Typical Sequence of Progression

Here is a typical sequence of progression for children when they are learning to use the toilet and transition out of diapers. It's a bit different for each child, but the sequence is a realistic rundown of what you might generally expect -- with regression and going forward again as a natural part of the process.

Whether you're just beginning or trying to start over, my typical scenario may help keep your expectations realistic. I also hope that it will help you take it one step at a time. Sometimes events such as taking trips or having visitors changes the child's routine and things go a little off course. You can use this scenario to see where you might want to get started from again (depending greatly on the child's age and other circumstances).

It's OK to begin a routine of trying on the toilet when your child is just 2 years old. But remember that at this very young age you are doing this for the sake of establishing a routine, not at all with the expectation that the child will progress quickly. The child will still be in diapers when you begin to establish the routine. Remove the diaper and allow the child to sit on the toilet, then put the diaper back on. Help the child learn the steps of the routine. Help with everything, including removing necessary clothing -- it helps keep the momentum going.

Many children learn to use the portable plastic potty, but I find that most children think of the plastic potty as a toy and seem to understand what the real toilet is for. They have to graduate to the real toilet eventually, so I like to provide a clip-on seat with a smaller hole and a step stool for their feet to rest on when they are seated on the real toilet. Their feet should not be dangling without any ability for leverage.

Steps in Progression

1. The child is about 2 years old, still in diapers, beginning to try routinely on the plastic potty or the real toilet (needs your help with EVERYTHING). Make the goal to TRY, not to actually go pee. Don't focus on bowel movements in the beginning.
2. The child learns the sequence of steps (actions) in the task, is still in diapers, is willing to try most of the time, but nothing happens most of the time.
3. The child starts to increasingly release pee in the potty (coincidentally at first), but is still in diapers.
4. The child starts to wear regular underwear sometimes, still in diapers most of the time (definitely for sleep). After experiencing accidents the child starts to realize that wearing wet clothing

is not what she wants. Increase times that she "tries" during the day.

5. The child increases times of wearing underwear during waking hours, maybe even skip diapers altogether during the day. There WILL be accidents! If we don't take them to "try", they will pee in their clothing.

6. At about 3 years old most children can stay dry from pee (out of diapers) but start to be resistant about pooping in the potty. It's okay to offer a diaper only for pooping if it helps, but do transition out of this eventually. More information on bowel movements in Chapter Seven.

 # THREE: QUESTIONS TO CONSIDER

Ask yourself these questions before beginning:

Is my child in the age range of 2 to 3 years old?
Between the second and third year, the child's body maturity and mentality are ready to begin learning the task. Children at this age can still be led a bit more easily than a four-year-old. I see it as a definite window of opportunity.

Do I expect my child to develop a bit more slowly than the "average" child, due to a special need?
A child with a disability can still benefit from the routine. For certain children, a slower pace or starting at an older age may be best.

What circumstances in our lives -- such as a new baby, moving, or beginning preschool -- may dictate when we begin the process ?
It's hard for children to deal with many big changes in their life at once. If you feel your child may have too many changes to get used to at once, you might want to introduce a consistent potty routine at a time when you know things will be predictable and consistent for at least 2 months or so. Every situation is different, but be mindful of how much change your child can handle.

Are you, the adult, feeling ready or ambivalent?
Children sense our emotional states. I think a child can sense the adult's ambivalence about following through with the toilet learning tasks and that's usually when the power struggles begin. Maybe the child gets nervous when he senses our nervousness. So try to be sure of your self and your decision to help your child go forward.

What should my attitude be like?
Try to have a calm and matter-of-fact attitude about the whole thing. Your attitude comes out in your voice, your eyes and looks, your own body tension, your speed of movement. Don't use sarcastic words or make comparisons like "don't you want to be a big boy like your friend?" or make threats like "you aren't going to be able to go to preschool unless you know how to use the potty". That may be somewhat true, but it's not helpful to say things like this to children. These types of messages are the very definition of "pushing a child."

Stay positive and be happy just that your child "tried," even if nothing was eliminated. Try not to get angry or punitive when the child is being resistant, or not releasing, or having accidents. Use language that says what CAN be done instead of what should not have been done. "Next time you can remember to let your pee go in the toilet instead of in your pants." Staying consistent with prompting and follow-through for your child is one big way that you show your attitude of encouragement and optimism.

What equipment will I need?

- Clip-on toilet seat (definitely), it's portable, some have soft sponge tops, easy to clean, safe with small hole, works on most real toilet; stool or platform for feet while sitting
- Plastic portable potty (maybe for long trips)
- Plastic shields to go over underwear (can be helpful)
- A potty "accident" kit (definitely)
- Tricks for the bathroom (definitely)
- Stickers or stamps for an immediate tangible reward (definitely)

FOUR: SIGNS OF READINESS

NOTE: Signs of readiness generally occur after at least 22 months of age.

Children express their interest through imitative behaviors

Imitation is a child's best way of learning something new. Young children quickly pick up on patterns that we follow in doing tasks and they begin to follow these patterns when the context of the situation fits. So if your child wants to pretend to use the potty just to copy you, cognitively it means the child probably understands that this is something we all do and that they can do it too. But that does not mean they can control their bodies yet.

Sitting ability and focus

If a child has the ability to sit and focus (be engaged) with a toy or book for about 10 to 15 minutes, this is a sign that their nervous systems are mature enough to deal with the potty training task. I DO NOT mean that I would make a child sit on a potty for 10 to 15 minutes. I simply mean that if a child can sit and focus for that amount of time, it's a sign that they are more mature in body and mind than a toddler (about 14 to 23 months of age). Toddlers are generally not ready to begin potty training.

Walking and running ability

Some 2-year-olds who have already started potty training are still mastering their running skills. You can see this development emerging when they are very physically active, running around and climbing on things a lot. Understand that gross motor tasks really takes over the child's thinking sometimes at this stage of development. At such times the child may not be interested in staying dry -- all they can think about is moving. This does not mean you stop going forward with the child, it just means you understand that the child's interests are not focused on staying dry. So you have to pay attention to their toileting needs for them.

Child wants to be changed when wet or soiled, likes to be neat and orderly

Being orderly or "neat" is part of the behavior that begins to appear from about 16 months to 2 years old. Children's brains are using patterns and recognizing correspondences and sometimes the neat and tidy behavior comes along with this. This has nothing to do with potty training. But these behaviors appear in the same time frame that many children begin to learn to use the toilet. This orderly, neat behavior (for instance, the child used to handle spaghetti but now wants clean hands) is a sign that the child is entering a new stage of maturity, and so learning how to use the potty may make more sense to the child now.

Negative behavior

Another age-related behavior that occurs around the time a child begins to learn to use the toilet is the typical demanding and frustrated behavior we often associated with two-year-olds. This is when your child wants something, you give it to her, then she doesn't want it, back and forth... leading to a meltdown. Kids naturally go through episodes like this. I advise to not introduce potty training when your child is in the middle of one of these stages. But if some negative behavior emerges months AFTER starting the process, you may have to just stay calm and keep following through to keep the routine consistent. When going through a negative patch don't expect as much from the child, but don't drop the routine either. That would give the wrong message. Remember that children can become extra strong-willed about the issues they intuitively feel they have control over: eating, sleeping, vocalizing, and eliminating.

 FIVE: THE DAILY
ROUTINE

**Make just "trying" the goal. Create a pattern of actions.
Focus on urination first.** Make the goal be just "trying".
Don't focus on actual elimination. Remember your child
may begin this process still wearing diapers most of the
time, because the first goal is to get the child used to just
trying without a fuss.

Children's brains are preprogrammed to follow patterns, like
routines, or repetition in language, etc. They don't choose
to follow such patterns, they are compelled to follow them.
Doing things over and over again in the same way (walking
to bathroom, removing their pants, sitting on potty, counting
to 20 or 30, wiping, replacing clothing, washing up) is part of
what helps them learn the task. *Take advantage of the child's
need to follow patterns.* One great way to help a child learn
to use the toilet is to establish a consistent pattern with the
routine.

Neural networks are formed by repetitive patterns of actions.
So following the same routine helps a child lay down the
neural networks to be masterful with the task as the pattern
is followed more and more.

Although many articles and books say the contrary, I believe that the great majority of children learn to stay dry from urine before they master pooping in the toilet. Some time between 3 and 3.5 years old children often start to resist using the toilet for pooping and seem to regress in general. This is when they are mastering their bowel movements. So, if your child is beginning the toilet learning process at 3 or 3.5, then they may be working on both developments at once. See Chapter Seven for more information on bowel movements. Concentrate on helping your child learn the pattern of actions it takes to follow through with the task of using the toilet and help your child focus on staying dry first.

Choose predictable times, and don't ask – make it a statement

Choose one to three predictable times during the day or evening when your child "tries" on the potty. These times should be attached to a predictable activity that happens in the routine of the day. Some examples to choose from are: in the morning when the night diaper is removed and new clothing is put on; before or after breakfast, lunch or dinner; before or after the evening bath or story time; or upon arrival home from preschool.

It's important to attach "bathroom times" with one of these very predictable activities during the day. You want to make it become part of the pattern of the day. The predictability of the two activities happening one after the other will help the child associate them with each other, making it easier to follow the pattern on his own as time goes by.

If you just randomly say it's time to try on the potty, whenever YOU want it to happen, the child is more likely to resist, and to not learn to feel the task as part of his normal routine. He also won't feel very autonomous. Making the effort to instill it into the routine sets the child up for more success. You will know you're on the right track if one day before lunch your child reminds you that bathroom time is supposed to happen before you eat and you are forgetting -- your child is reminded of it because it is part of the pattern you have established before lunch takes place. I have a lot of faith in the power of this strategy.

Help them with everything: prompting, undressing, sitting on the potty

Bathroom times must be on your agenda too. The adult must prompt and initiate most of the time. They need you to keep the routine going. Also, don't expect your child to always remove their clothing and put it back on properly when using the toilet. My advice is to just help with the child's clothing. Sometimes you have a lot of momentum going in the right direction. The child is going along with the program so willingly, then you ask them to remove their pants and they put up a fuss and the momentum goes away. If we help them with their clothing during toileting times (which can make the whole thing go more smoothly) they will still learn to dress and undress themselves on their own, don't worry.

Dress children in easy-to-remove clothing. Stay away from suspenders, buttons, buckles, zippers, etc. Keep it simple with elastic waistbands and velcro closures.

You can deal with the child's clothing, then lift them up and place them on the toilet seat. Another good approach is to get a step stool so the child can climb up and sit on the potty independently. We not only have to help them with their clothing but we also need to get them used to sitting there for at least 20 to 30 seconds.

Counting to 10, 20, or 30 is a very effective trick

As soon as the child is seated on the potty, begin to count to 10 or 20 in a positive, rhythmic way, not too fast and not too slow. Your child is very tuned into such patterns. Counting is thus compelling for the brain to want to pay attention to and complete the pattern once it begins. The young child's "single focus" on the pattern of the numbers is a natural part of how the brain is functioning at that age. Counting to 10 or 20 gives the child's brain and body a chance to get used to this part of the toileting task, which is, just sitting on the potty for about 20 to 30 seconds. The child will begin to look forward to counting and repeat the numbers along with you instead of bolting off the toilet as soon as you put him on it. The child is not only getting practice with the sequence of the numbers and their names, but he is also getting used to the routine without feeling pressured. It's a bit of a trick on his brain but it certainly does not harm and it really does help! (Some other effective tricks are provided in the next section.)

The counting ritual also helps the adult remember to NOT make the child sit on the toilet for a long time in the hope that something will be produced. When we insist that a child stay on the toilet for a long time (more than 30 seconds) it usually makes the child feel that they do not like the task and they feel forced. Sometimes this makes them hold it in more and resist. If the child is the one that initiates sitting longer, that is different and OK.

Rewards and praise

Let's start with rewards. There is no need to offer candy or toys for sitting on the potty or eliminating. Promises of future activities or outings are not very helpful either in motivating your child to use the potty. Young children are usually in the moment. They can't help it. More effective rewards for this age range are tangible, immediate and simple, like a stamp or sticker for the hand just for trying on the potty.

Blowing a round of bubbles in the bathroom after trying is also a great reward. And that bubble maker must stay in the bathroom in a special spot. If it is taken out of the bathroom it will lose its power as a reward for trying on the potty. Keep it associated only with the bathroom.

If we don't help them follow through, they will have accidents

Remember that young children get very single minded on what they are paying attention to in a given moment. So they need adults to help them regulate their bathroom use: building in times to use the bathroom helps them learn how to do it on their own as they mature. It becomes a habit in a way.

A habit you can help instill in girls is to wipe after toileting from front to back.

Teach girls to do it this way to keep bacteria from being spread into the urinary tract.

How long does potty training go on?

Children, that are developing typically, begin practice with the toilet at about 2.5 years old and can usually wear regular underwear during the day by about age 3. Most children go through a regression period around 3 to 3.5 years old with respect to the issue of bowel movements, but they get over it and usually never need to use diapers again. Children often start to wake up in the morning with a dry diaper at about 4.5 years old. Diapers are commonly used for nighttime sleep, sometimes until 5 years old. Every child is different.

SIX: TRICKS THAT MOTIVATE

We need tricks and techniques to help the child with initiating and following through. I always say we have to have lots of tricks up our sleeves when it comes to dealing with young children. The following techniques are the ones I know work with potty training, if you use them in the prescribed way. When I need a little help in getting the child to go along agreeably, these help tremendously. I do not feel that these strategies are mere distractions -- I believe they help us build the pattern for the child.

It's important to keep the "trick" in the bathroom. If you allow the child to take it out of the bathroom it will lose its ability to be a good trick. You give it even more power if you keep it in a spot where only you can access it.

Use one trick at a time, and only one trick a week. Change to a new one the next week, but put the previous one away, out of sight. This way you will be rotating a small collection of tricks, which keeps the novelty high and actually works for you in many ways. Children like novelty but they also like repetition; it's a tangible thing, and it takes their mind off of getting into a power struggle around using the potty. And they enjoy the trick so it grows on itself and teaches children all kinds of things unrelated to potty training!

"Search and Find" game

Here's one example: get an image of a ladybug (a cutout, or you can draw it yourself and cut it out), then, using tape, stick it on the top of the bathroom mirror or somewhere that the child cannot reach. Tell the child a story about the ladybug (or whatever it is, you could even have two different creatures). The story has to be very short and always the same so a pattern gets established. Before it's time to try on the potty, you secretly move the lady bug to another spot so the child will be compelled to go in the bathroom and look for it, this helps you do the next step which is to talk about the story and help him with his clothing and follow through. They not only look forward to it, it stimulates learning through the "Search and Find" game and the story's language-building qualities. It helps you distract from power struggles while it also helps steer the child into the routine.

Animal figurines

Very similar to the "Search and Find" game, create a very brief story with two small animal figurines. Keep them in a special place in the bathroom. These do not get used in a "search and find" way. They are simply taken out and used when trying on the potty and put away when it is over. These can be helpful when the child begins to have BMs on the toilet. They like to sit for a while as they tell themselves the story.

Bubbles

Keep a small container of bubbles with a wand in the bathroom. It's a good post- potty-time reward. Or it can be the thing that gets them into the bathroom; then you can help them follow through with potty time while they enjoy the bubbles.

Favorite children's picture book page on the wall

You can get a color copy of a page or two of a favorite children's picture book. I like to have them laminated too. Hang one on the wall near the toilet. It gives the child something fun to look at while using the toilet. It also provides lots of opportunities for practicing language, including talking about the picture book it came from or identifying specific images on the page.

A new book

You can borrow books from the library or buy a small set of books that you NEVER use for any other purpose. Only use them in the bathroom. Rotate one book in and out per week.

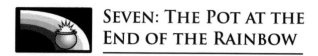

SEVEN: THE POT AT THE END OF THE RAINBOW

The following story may sound familiar, or it may have more meaning when your child gets to what I humerously call the last stage, "the end of the rainbow".

Regression around bowel movements, and sometimes urinating too, seems to be a phase that almost all children go through. For girls, it generally happens around age 3, and boys around 3.5. After being able to stay dry quite well for many months the child starts to hold their bowel movements and some get very constipated in the process. Many children ask to wear the diaper and as soon as they get it on, they have a bowel movement. But if you notice that they have to have a bowel movement and hurry them to the toilet, they can no longer go. The urge has gone away and it feels frustrating and physically uncomfortable for the child.

When your child gets to this part of the process, try the following three-step strategy to help the child gradually learn to consistently have their bowel movements on the toilet.

Example: let's consider a child who attends preschool and does not have bowel movements there. The child always has his bowel movements at home, soon after arriving home from preschool. I use this example because many children are like this.

Step One: Using a diaper

Even if the child has only been wearing diapers for night sleeping, you can go back to using diapers for bowel movements ONLY.

Right after getting home from preschool put a diaper on the child. Explain that he can play for a while and if he needs to poop, he can go in the diaper. Tell him you will then clean him up and put his underwear back on.

Give him time to play, 30 minutes or more. When the child plays and is very relaxed, his body gets into the "zone" and he can release his bowel movement. Do not disturb him. There is no need to tell him that you know what he is doing. Give him his privacy. Clean him up directly after he is finished. Even if he denies he has gone. They do that.

This step helps the child get used to being aware of the need to go, concentrating on releasing it, and going through the discomfort of releasing it without interuption. This is the mind-body connection that children are still mastering. This is the thing we disrupt when we hurry them to the toilet. We take them out of the zone and they can't learn how to work their own body. I know, "they have been pooping since Day One." Yes, it's true. But never have they done it with such awareness about needing to do it in the right place and that no one wants to soil their clothing, and so forth.

After doing Step One for about 2 weeks you can go to step two.

Step Two: Must be in the bathroom

Now that the child has had time to master how to release with more awareness, you can now say that when you notice he has to go, you will take him to the bathroom. Disable the lock on the bathroom door so you can say he can close it to have privacy. Tell him that he can still poop in his diaper but he must come into the bathroom to do it. Provide bubbles or something else to use in the bathroom so he can focus on making the bubbles instead of the bowel movement. That will help him get himself back into the zone and release. And now he will be in the right place too. You're creating a habit to go into the bathroom when the feeling comes on, laying down the neural pathways for that pattern of actions when the urge comes on.

When he is done, immediately go in and clean him up and put the underwear back on. After a few weeks, you may decide to move to step three.

Step Three: No more diapers

Now it's time to say no more diapers. The child has had time to practice, step by step, getting to this point. You have respectfully provided the help in a 3-step process. He knows how to recognize the urge. He knows how to transfer himself into the bathroom and get privacy. He knows how to sit on the potty and his clothes are easy to deal with (and you may go in and help him with his clothes and onto the seat and get him set up with a "trick" to focus on). The rest is totally up to him. He has to get back in the "zone" but he has had the "training" he needs to succeed. Again, the rest is up to the child.

Laxatives and stool softeners

It's common for a child to get constipated during the last phase of learning to use the toilet. To recognize the urge and then stay on task to get to the correct place, a toilet, is simply not first on a young child's agenda. So they hold their BMs and when asked to produce they just can't. There are certainly more reasons why children get constipated, such as a poor diet, but generally, being constipated is a step on the way to mastering the bowel movement. It seems to be a predictable part of the process.

Sometimes a pediatrician will give you a laxative to help the child get "cleared out". Or else a stool softener may be prescribed. It is important to relieve the child, but equally important is to discontinue the medication after the "clearing" has taken place. I have talked to many parents who thought the stool softener or laxative was helping the child avoid constipation in an on-going way, only causing loose stools all the time. Making the child anxious of poop accidents.

This is what I think happens and why I think it's best to use the medication to help clear the child's intestines, but then stop the medication and replace the needed flora in

the child's digestive system. Then give the digestive tract a chance to normalize.

Laxatives, if constantly in the child's system can flush out a lot of good natural intestinal flora. It often makes the child feel like they have uncontrollable diarrhea because their stools are too loose, and this creates anxiety.

If things are like this for the child, I wonder if his/her brain is just laying down neural networks to deal with "holding it in" instead of feeling how to release it at the right place at the right time.

Once the child's system is cleared, stop the medication and give the child something with acidophilus (probiotics) and avoid sugars. There are yogurts, yogurt drinks, milks etc. The natural flora help stools to be released easily but in solid form.

EIGHT: DEVELOPMENT EBBS AND FLOWS

Regression is a part of progression. We often take a few steps back after we have taken a giant leap forward. Children operate this way too. Any time there is a big change in the child's life, regression in one form or another may occur.

Here are some common situations when you may see regression in your child's potty training.

1. The child moves out of the crib and into a real bed, or a new bedroom.
2. The security blanket has been phased out, or pacifiers, bottles, etc.
3. A parent is away for a while, or a new person comes to live with you, a guest who stays for more than just a day or so.
4. Any break in the routine can cause a regression. Illness, moving to a new environment, starting preschool or getting a new babysitter can also trigger regression.

You cannot stop or prevent regression from occurring. Regression actually seems to help children move forward even further. So take the regressions in stride, just help the child get back on track. In time the child's physical and mental maturity will take care of the rest.

NINE: GOING TO PRESCHOOL

When going to preschool, success in potty training is imminent. Many children between ages 2 and 3 are still challenged by the whole task of learning to use the toilet. But they master it quickly, once they start participating in a preschool program. Children who have had practice at home, even if they have not been totally successful, are much more able to transfer the skills to preschool.

Consistency

Parents and preschool teachers often strive to provide consistency with methods, strategies, and rewards to help the child become independent with using the toilet.

But let's face it…children behave differently with their teachers than they do with their parents. Young children are much more willing to be steered into doing certain things by their teachers. There is generally less rebellion and more cooperation.

It does not matter who the parent is, the best parent on the planet will not get the consistent cooperation from the child that the preschool teacher will (granted he/she is a great teacher). It's just the typical way things go. So if you give your children a jump-start by providing some practice at home, they will probably progress very quickly in their ability to take care of themselves with toileting once they get to preschool.

Supportive teachers

You can think of learning to use the toilet independently as part of the preschool curriculum. It's part of learning to understand one's own body and how to take care of it. Some preschools ask that children be potty trained before they enter the program. Some will say it does not matter whether the child is potty trained or not. Some preschools have parents return to the school if the child has a toileting

accident so the parent can take care of the child and clean things up. Other schools will take care of toileting accidents on their own and consider it as part of what children are learning. So, it's important to choose a school that will support you in the way you need to be supported.

A helpful teacher will talk to you about nurturing the child's progress and how you can do that at school and at home. Children catch on quickly at preschool because they want to do what everyone else is doing. Copying is one of the easiest ways young children learn. The preschool program is structured around a daily routine, and since children are hard wired to follow patterns (the routine of the day is a pattern) their practice with using the toilet builds up, so they achieve some mastery at a fast pace.

When observing a preschool class of 2 year olds, it's not unusual to see a systematic restroom break for the kids every 30-45 minutes. Because younger children need more individual attention in the restroom, I don't like to see the "herding mentality" when the restroom break occurs. The herding mentality is when all kids are made to stop playing and get in-line for their turn in the restroom. This only creates difficulties of many sorts.

It's much better to take a few children to the restroom at a time, give them guidance, make sure they wash their hands and then get a few more children until the whole group has gone through the cycle. Skilled teachers know how to transition children in and out of restroom breaks with out disrupting the whole group.

Accidents at preschool

Almost all children have at least one toileting accident at preschool. Here are some tips to help:

1. Keep a supply of extra clothes for your child at preschool. Mark them with your child's name. Take pants, shirts, underwear, socks and an extra pair of shoes.

2. Have your child wear a diaper under a pair of underwear for the journey to preschool in the morning, upon arriving at preschool, take your child to the bathroom and remove the diaper (without taking off the underwear) and just pull the underwear back up. You can do the reverse for the trip home.

3. Remember that naptime is when your child may have an accident because their bladder control gets much weaker when they are asleep.

4. It's important to bath your child nightly when they are attending preschool, not only do they get dirty from playing, they also have toileting accidents.

5. Don't act surprised or disappointed when your child brings home a bag of soiled clothes. Be "matter of fact" and encourage them to try to do better next time.

Never shame or demean the child about the accident. It never helps. It sometimes makes things worse.

It's also shaming to many children to be told that their eliminations are yucky or gross or stinky, Again try to speak matter-of-factly and stay even-toned.

A good preschool will make a big difference in your child's desire to progress with the toileting task. Get your child on a helpful routine with potty training at home and the preschool experience will help your child continue on to full success.

BEST WISHES

Helping your child learn to use the toilet is a memory you may not retain. When it's over, you will be moving on to other things and so will your child. And even though the task isn't the most fun you have ever had, it is one of the biggest leaps of independence you will help your child make while they are this young. So pay attention and savor this special and fleeting time. Just keep in mind that ALL children are different, even twins, and each one will develop in their own way. It's important to give each one the space and time to mature while also providing them with the right environment, guidance, and attitude to help them succeed. I hope this book helps you to do just that.

Printed in the United States
By Bookmasters